THEA
TRVM
ORBIS
TERRA
RVM

Opus nunc denuo ab ipso Auctore recognitum, multisque locis castigatum, & quamplurimis
nouis Tabulis atque Commentarijs auctum.

Pomegranate Artbooks • San Francisco

MAPS

OF THE

ANCIENT

WORLD

A BOOK
OF
POSTCARDS

Pomegranate Artbooks
Box 6099
Rohnert Park, CA 94927

ISBN 1-56640-966-7
Pomegranate Catalog No. A713

Pomegranate publishes books of postcards on a variety of subjects.
Please write to the publisher for more information.

Title page: *Theatrum Orbis Terrarum*, Abraham Ortelius, Antwerp, 1570/1595. This is the actual title page from the 1595 edition of the first modern atlas, originally published in 1570. Allegorical figures representing the continents depict a regal and dominant Europe (top) and subservient Asia (left), Africa (right) and America (bottom). The Indian maiden representing America holds a severed head in her hand, reflecting the belief that cannibalism was practiced in the New World.

ARGONAVTICA.

EVRO-PAE PA-RS

PARS

SCYTHAE

GETAE. ARIMASTHEI

SAVROMATAE

Immensa silva

HYPERBO-REI. SCYTHAE.

BASTARNAE.

GELO-NES

ALANI.

Mirace

MAEOTIS PALVS.

ARSOPAE.

MACETAE

GRAVCENII.

Ishylus

CECRYPHAE.

PARS

CELTAE.

LIGVRES

EVRO-PAE

CRO-NIVM MARE

TAVRICA.

CHARANDAE.

DIALERES

OMYNI

CAVCASEVM MARE.

BVONOMAE

MENICOCHI.

COL

CHIS.

ENCHELEAE.

NESTAEI.

AXENVM Aequor, Iasonio
pulsatum remige primum

LATIVM.

TVRRHE-NIA.

SINDI

SARDO-VM

PELA-GVS.

AVSO-NIA.

CORALLI

THRACIA.

ASSYRII.

PAPHLA-GONIA.

CHALYBES.

TIBARE-NIA.

MOSINOECI.

CAPPA-DOCIA.

MACRONES.

AMAZO-NES.

Doeantis, siue
Boeantis campus.

RECHI-REI.

MOSCHI.

Cytaica regio.

CHIS.

TYRRHENVM AEQVOR.

TRINACRIA.

IONIVM MARE.

THESSA-LIA.

ACHAIA.

PELOPIS REGIO.

MINOIVM

Pelagus

Minoi des
insulae.

Sporades insulae.

DICTAEVM Mar.

MAVRI.

BEBRYCIA.

ASIAE

PARS

THESSA-LIA.

DO-LOPES.

MAGNE-SIA.

PELASGIA.

AEMONIA.

LOCRI.

Minoium
pelagus

LIBYSTICVM MARE.

CRETA.

Carpathus.

THRACIAE PARS.

PROPON-TIS.

BEBRY-CIA.

CYANEA Re-

Mc-las fl.

DOLIONES

MYSIA.

BITHYNIA.

BARDA-NIA.

Ex conatibus Geographicis Abrahami Ortelij Antverp.

Syrtes, siue mare
vadosum ac arenosum.

ATLANTICVS Ager.

Hesperides.

SACER Campus

MERIDIES.

CYRENE

LIBYAE

PARS.

MAPS OF THE ANCIENT WORLD

JASON AND THE ARGONAUTS

Abraham Ortelius, in *Parergon*, Antwerp, 1598
Smith Collection, University of Southern Maine

Seen here are the regions traversed by Jason and the Argonauts
on their successful quest to capture the Golden Fleece from the
king of Colchis on the far eastern shore of the Black Sea
(CAVCASEVM MARE). In the vignette below the title, the Golden
Fleece is seen hanging from a tree, guarded by a dragon and two
fire-breathing bulls.

Pomegranate; Box 6099, Rohnert Park, CA 94927

These postcards display images of the ancient world in the form of maps produced between 1475 and 1854. They consequently embody concepts of geography and history spanning almost 400 years, from the Renaissance to the modern period. On examination, it is apparent that these are more than decorative geographic delineations of the ancient world. They are, in fact, works of art whose imagery and inscriptions serve the dual purposes of adorning and informing. Against the backdrop of their geographic locales, scriptural, historical and mythological characters and events are graphically portrayed by means of vignettes, inscriptions and explanatory tables. The result is an aesthetically pleasing and extraordinarily effective means of visual communication.

Most of the maps reproduced here were made by the great Flemish cartographer Abraham Ortelius (1527–1598), who is perhaps best known as the author of the first modern atlas. Published in 1570, his *Theatrum Orbis Terrarum* was the first map book to provide comprehensive and systematic coverage of the entire known world with maps of uniform format, an arrangement that has been followed to the present day. The *Theatrum* was an enormous geographic and commercial success; more than thirty editions containing increasing numbers of maps were published in seven languages over a forty-two-year span. An antiquarian himself, Ortelius incrementally added maps of lands of the Bible and classical civilizations to editions of the *Theatrum* beginning in 1579, eventually constituting a separate classical atlas called the *Parergon*. The maps seen here are from the 1595 editions of the *Theatrum* and *Parergon*, with the exception of *Jason and the Argonauts*, which appeared in the 1598 *Parergon*.

The maps reproduced in this book are drawn from the collections of the Osher Map Library of the University of Southern Maine. They represent a small sampling of the estimated 20,000 maps contained in two major holdings, the Smith and Osher Collections. This number includes both individual sheet maps and those bound in approximately 600 atlases, geographies, histories and related volumes. There are, in addition, more than seventy-five terrestrial and celestial globes and a collection of specialized reference works. Materials in the combined collections span a period of more than five centuries. The Osher Map Library constitutes a significant resource for teaching and research in the history of cartography and in a number of other disciplines, including geography, history, art, anthropology and technological and cultural development. The recently completed facilities include an exhibition gallery open to the public free of charge.

PEREGRINATIONIS DIVI PAVLI TYPVS COROGRAPHICVS.

In quo et noui testamenti, in primis autem apostolorum historiae, à sancto Luca descriptae, omnia fere loca geographica, oculis inspicienda, exhibentur.

MARIS MEDITERRANEI PARS

Abrah. Ortelius describebat 1579

MAPS OF THE ANCIENT WORLD

THE TRAVELS OF SAINT PAUL

Abraham Ortelius, in *Parergon*, Antwerp, 1595

Osher Collection, University of Southern Maine

This map depicts the regions traversed by Saint Paul during his wide-ranging missionary activities, extending from Italy to Mesopotamia. Beautifully executed vignettes flanking the title cartouche illustrate episodes from the life of Saint Paul. On the left his conversion to Christianity is dramatically portrayed; on the right he is shown shipwrecked on the island of Malta en route to his trial in Rome.

Pomegranate, Box 6099, Rohnert Park, CA 94927

MAPS OF THE ANCIENT WORLD

PALESTINE

Lucas Brandis, in *Rudimentum Novitiorum*,
Lubeck, 1475

Osher Collection, University of Southern Maine

This is the first modern printed map. East is at the top, and
cities and regions are depicted as stylized hills, with Jerusalem
at the center. Crude illustrations of biblical scenes include Moses
receiving the Tablets of the Law on Mount Sinai (top right corner),
the submerged cities of Sodom and Gomorrah protruding from
the Dead Sea (upper right), the Baptism of Jesus (upper center)
and the Crucifixion (below Jerusalem).

Pomegranate: Box 6099, Rohnert Park, CA 94927

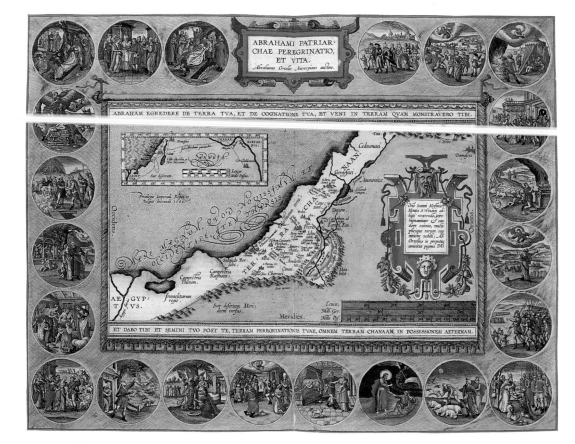

ABRAHAMI PATRIAR=
CHAE PEREGRINATIO,
ET VITA.
Abrahamo Ortelio Antverpiano auctore.

ABRAHAM EGREDERE DE TERRA TVA, ET DE COGNATIONE TVA, ET VENI IN TERRAM QVAM MONSTRAVERO TIBI.

Privilegio Imperiali, Regio, et
Belgico decennale 1586.

MARE MAGNVM, QVOD NOVISSIMVM, ET
OCCIDENTALE ITEM DICITVR IMERSIS

AEGYP=
TVS.

Israelitarum
regno.

Sur desertum Meri-
diem versus.   Meridies.

ET DABO TIBI ET SEMINI TVO POST TE, TERRAM PEREGRINATIONIS TVAE, OMNEM TERRAM CHANAAN, IN POSSESSIONEM AETERNAM.

MAPS OF THE ANCIENT WORLD

ABRAHAM THE PATRIARCH

Abraham Ortelius, in *Parergon*, Antwerp, 1595
Osher Collection, University of Southern Maine

This map is considered one of Ortelius's masterpieces. The map itself is in the form of a tapestry depicting the land of Canaan with its ancient tribal divisions, surrounded by twenty-two medallion scenes illustrating the life of Abraham the Patriarch. A small inset map traces his wanderings from the Euphrates Valley to the Promised Land.

Pomegranate, Box 6099, Rohnert Park, CA 94927

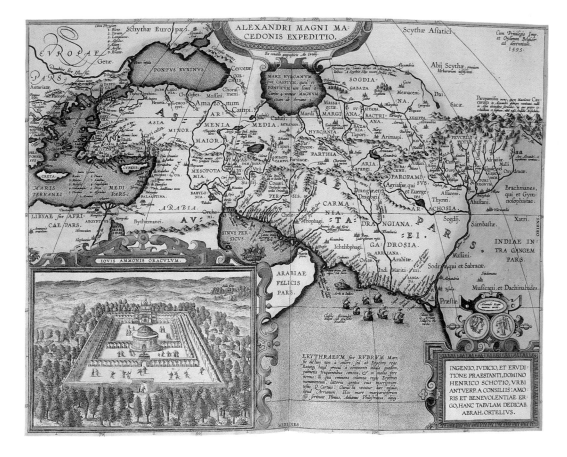

MAPS OF THE ANCIENT WORLD

THE CONQUESTS OF ALEXANDER THE GREAT

Abraham Ortelius, in *Parergon*, Antwerp, 1595
Osher Collection, University of Southern Maine

This map depicts the vast area conquered by the young
Macedonian king Alexander the Great, extending eastward from
Byzantium and Egypt to the Indus River. An inset in the lower left
corner presents a finely engraved bird's-eye view of the oracle of
Zeus at Ammon, Egypt. Surmounting the dedication cartouche at
the lower right is an engraving of a gold coin bearing the helmet-
ed likeness of Alexander.

Pomegranate, Box 6099, Rohnert Park, CA 94927

MAPS OF THE ANCIENT WORLD

THE ANCIENT ROMAN EMPIRE

Abraham Ortelius, in *Parergon*, Antwerp, 1595
Osher Collection, University of Southern Maine

The elegant design of this map complements the geographic
delineation with embellishments illustrating the history of the
Roman Empire. These include medallion portraits of Romulus
and Remus, a text panel containing a brief history of the Roman
Empire, and a genealogical diagram of the lineage of the Roman
emperors.

Pomegranate, Box 6099, Rohnert Park, CA 94927

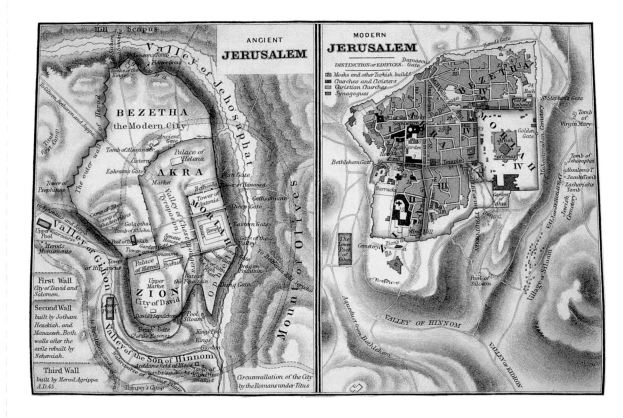

MAPS OF THE ANCIENT WORLD

ANCIENT JERUSALEM/MODERN JERUSALEM

Lyman Coleman, in . . . *Text Book and Atlas of Biblical Geography*, Philadelphia, 1854

Osher Collection, University of Southern Maine

This is the frontispiece of a popular nineteenth-century biblical geography book designed to call attention to "a most important but neglected branch of education." "Modern Jerusalem" is actually the old walled city as it existed in the mid-nineteenth century. Many important holy sites are identified, including the ancient Temple, the Church of the Holy Sepulchre, the Mosque of Omar and the "Wailing Wall."

Pomegranate, Box 6099, Rohnert Park, CA 94927

MAPS OF THE ANCIENT WORLD

PALESTINE

Johann Christoph Harenberg
in Composite Atlas, 1700–1760
Smith Collection, University of Southern Maine

Although this eighteenth-century map is more scientific in design, it retains many of the traditional features of earlier maps of the Holy Land. The route of the Exodus is shown, along with the tribal divisions, "extended by King David and Solomon."

Pomegranate, Box 6099, Rohnert Park, CA 94927

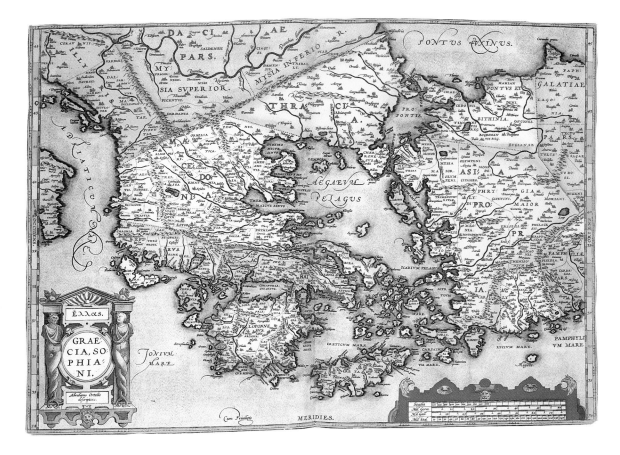

MAPS OF THE ANCIENT WORLD

THE ANCIENT GREEK WORLD

Abraham Ortelius, in *Parergon*, Antwerp, 1595
Osher Collection, University of Southern Maine

This map portrays ancient Greece, with its independent city-states
and kingdoms and their provinces extending from the Balkan
Peninsula through the Ionian, Mediterranean and Aegean seas
to Asia Minor. The name of the country, Ellas, is displayed in
Greek letters on the lintel of the architectural cartouche in the
lower left corner.

Pomegranate; Box 6099, Rohnert Park, CA 94927

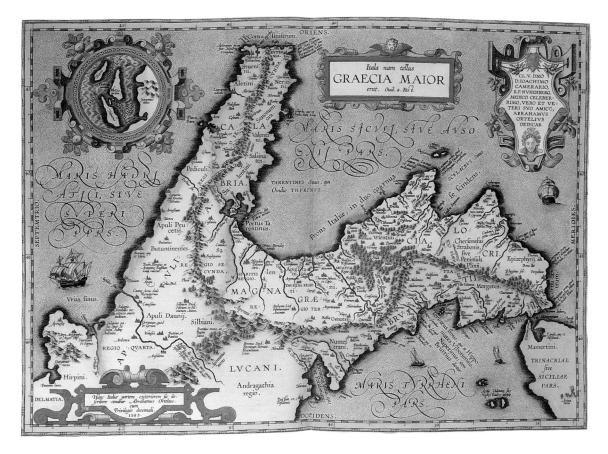

MAPS OF THE ANCIENT WORLD

ANCIENT GREEK COLONIES IN ITALY

Abraham Ortelius, in *Parergon*, Antwerp, 1595

Osher Collection, University of Southern Maine

This map, oriented with east at the top, shows the ancient
Greek seaport colonies in southern Italy, known as Magna
Graecia. Major cities included Tarentum, Croton and Heraclea.
The latter was the site of the famous battle in which Pyrrhus,
king of Epirus, sustained devastating losses in defeating the
Romans, giving rise to the term "Pyrrhic victory."

Pomegranate, Box 6099, Rohnert Park, CA 94927

MAPS OF THE ANCIENT WORLD

ANCIENT TUSCANY

Abraham Ortelius, in *Parergon*, Antwerp, 1595
Osher Collection, University of Southern Maine

This map depicts the central Italian region of Etruria, later named
Tuscany, home of the ancient Etruscans. Believed to have
migrated from Asia Minor, the Etruscans were successful traders
who built a number of cities, among them Florence, and
developed an advanced civilization noted for its art. Etruria was
eventually defeated by and annexed to Rome.

Pomegranate, Box 6099, Rohnert Park, CA 94927

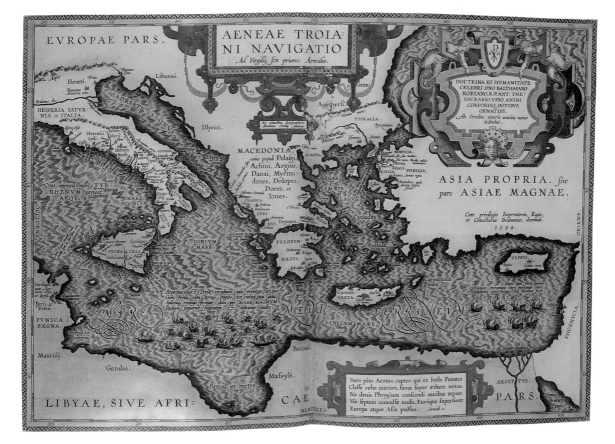

EVROPAE PARS.

AENEAE TROIA-
NI NAVIGATIO
Ad Virgilij, sex priores Aeneidos.

Ex conatibus Geographicis
Abrahami Ortelij Antverp.

DOCTRINA ET HVMANITATE
CELEBRI DNO BALTHASARO
ROBIANO, R.P. ANT. THE-
SAVRARIO, VIRO ANIMI
CORPORISQ. DOTIBVS
ORNATISS.
Ab Ortelius veteris amicitiæ memor
dedicabat.

ASIA PROPRIA. sive
pars ASIAE MAGNAE.

Cum privilegio Imperatorio, Regio,
et Cancellariæ Brabantiæ, decennali.
1594.

HESPERIA SATVR-
NIA et ITALIA.

HADRIATICVS SINVS.

Illyrici.

Illyricum

MACEDONIA,
cuius populi Pelasgi,
Achiui, Argiui,
Danai, Myrmi-
dones, Dolopes,
Dores, et
Iones.

THRACIA.

Gens inimica mihi TYR
RHENVM nauigat
AEQVOR

MARE
AVSONIVM

AEGAE
VM MARE

PELAGVS

Cyclades

OCCIDENS.

IONIVM
MARE.

PELOPON-
NESVS

insula

ORIENS.

TRINA CRIA

CYPRVS.

Septima post Troiæ excidium, iam vertitur Æstas:
Cum freta, cum terras omnes, toe vbiui freta sacta,
Syteruq. emensæ ferremur, & dum per MARE MAGNVM
Italiam sequimur fugientes; Voluimur vndis.

Curetes.
CRETA.

Carpathium
mare.

MARE   MEDI   TERRA   NEVM

LIBYCVM MARE.

PICENTIA.

PVNICA
REGNA.

Maurisij.

Getulae.

Massyli.

Breuia, et Syrtes.

Barcaei.

AEGYPTVS.
PARS.

LIBYAE, SIVE AFRI=   CAE

MERIDIES.

Sum pius Aeneas, raptos qui ex hoste Penates
Classe veho mecum, fama super æthera notus.
Bis denis Phrygium conscendi nauibus æquor,
Vix septem conuulsæ undis, Europ̄q superstant:
Europa atque Asia pulsus.   Aeneid. 1.

MAPS OF THE ANCIENT WORLD

THE VOYAGE OF AENEAS

Abraham Ortelius, in *Parergon*, Antwerp, 1595
Osher Collection, University of Southern Maine

This map illustrates the voyage of Aeneas as recounted in Virgil's
epic poem, the *Aeneid*. Following the destruction of Troy by the
Greeks, Aeneas, a Trojan prince and son of the goddess Venus,
embarked on an adventurous voyage, finally reaching Italy and
becoming the legendary founder of the Roman people.

Pomegranate, Box 6099, Rohnert Park, CA 94927

MAPS OF THE ANCIENT WORLD

ANCIENT ITALY

Abraham Ortelius, in *Parergon*, Antwerp, 1595
Osher Collection, University of Southern Maine

This map depicts the entire peninsula of ancient Italy, with a
detailed portrayal of topographic features such as coastlines,
rivers, lakes and mountains. Political subdivisions are named,
and cities are indicated by red symbols in the form of buildings
or groups of buildings, the size of the symbol being proportional
to the size of the city. A decorative cartouche at the lower center
contains imagery from Italian history and mythology.

Pomegranate, Box 6099, Rohnert Park, CA 94927

MAPS OF THE ANCIENT WORLD
LATIUM

Abraham Ortelius, in *Parergon*, Antwerp, 1595
Osher Collection, University of Southern Maine

This map depicts the central region of Italy inhabited by the
ancient Latins. A miniature plan of the walled city of Rome is
seen at its western border. An inset view at the lower left depicts
the Circaean Promontory, described in the *Aeneid* as the home of
the enchantress Circe, who changed the companions of Odysseus
into swine.

Pomegranate, Box 6099, Rohnert Park, CA 94927

MAPS OF THE ANCIENT WORLD

THE GREAT FLOOD . . . SONS OF NOAH
Maker unknown; from a Dutch Bible
[seventeenth century]

Smith Collection, University of Southern Maine

This Bible map encompasses a large region of the Near East, from Cilicia and Egypt in the east to Assyria and Nod in the west. It is designed to illustrate the account of the Great Flood in the third chapter of Genesis and the subsequent repopulation of the world by the three sons of Noah. The anti-Papal iconography at the top marks this as being from a Protestant Bible.

Pomegranate, Box 6099, Rohnert Park, CA 94927

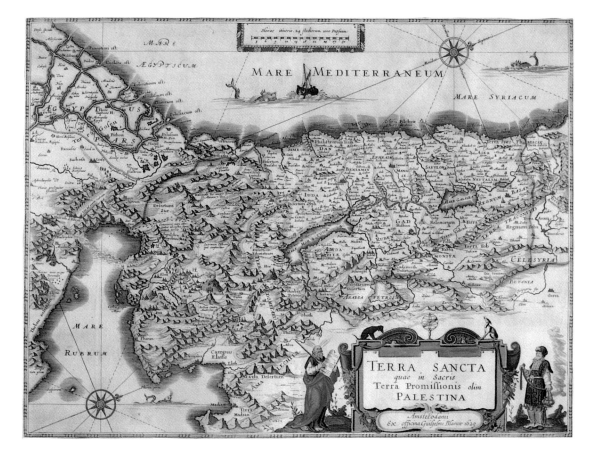

Horae itineris 24 stadiorum 1000 Passum

MARE ÆGYPTISCUM

MARE MEDITERRANEUM

MARE SYRIACUM

ÆGYPTUS

GOLFO DI PARS

Terra SYR. PHOENICIÆ

SIMEON · DAN

Philistæorum Terra

EPHRAIM

BENIAMIN

MANASSE

SABULON

NEPTALI

Lacus GALILÆ

REGNUM BASAN

IUDA

GAD

ISSACHAR

REGNUM Zeb.

RUBEN

TRACHONITI

Terra Tob

CÆLESYRIA

MOABITA

MONITA

BATANIA

ARABIA PETRÆA

IDUMÆA

MARE RUBRUM

Desertum Zur

Desertum Zin

Campus Elathis

Zipha Desertum

Terra Madian

TERRA SANCTA
quae in Sacris
Terra Promissionis olim
PALESTINA

Amstelodami
Ex officina Gulielmi Blaeuw 1629

MAPS OF THE ANCIENT WORLD

HOLY LAND

Willem Janszoon Blaeu

from Joan Blaeu, *Grooten Atlas*, 1664

Osher Collection, University of Southern Maine

The Exodus from Egypt, the crossing of the Red Sea, and the wanderings of the Children of Israel are seen here, along with tiny vignettes and legends chronicling the events en route. With west at the top, the Holy Land is presented as it would have appeared to the Israelites approaching from the east. The title cartouche is flanked by figures of Moses holding the Sacred Tablets and Aaron garbed as the High Priest.

Pomegranate, Box 6099, Rohnert Park, CA 94927

MAPS of the ANCIENT WORLD

ANCIENT EGYPT

Abraham Ortelius, in *Parergon*, Antwerp, 1595
Osher Collection, University of Southern Maine

This map is oriented with east at the top, allowing a detailed
rendering of the Nile River and its delta across the width of the
map. The inset view of Alexandria at the upper right shows its
system of canals and the peninsula of Pharos, site of the great
lighthouse, one of the Seven Wonders of the Ancient World.

Pomegranate, Box 6099, Rohnert Park, CA 94927

GALLIA

VETVS,

Ad Iulij Cæsaris commentaria:
ex Conatibus geographicis
Abrah. Ortelij
1590.

MAPS OF THE ANCIENT WORLD

CAESAR'S GAUL

Abraham Ortelius, in *Parergon*, Antwerp, 1595
Osher Collection, University of Southern Maine

Ancient Gaul is depicted here in accordance with the description
in Julius Caesar's *Commentaria*, one of the earliest works to
have historical maps created for it. Major topographic features
and locations of native tribes, cities and Roman provinces are
indicated.

Pomegranate, Box 6099, Rohnert Park, CA 94927

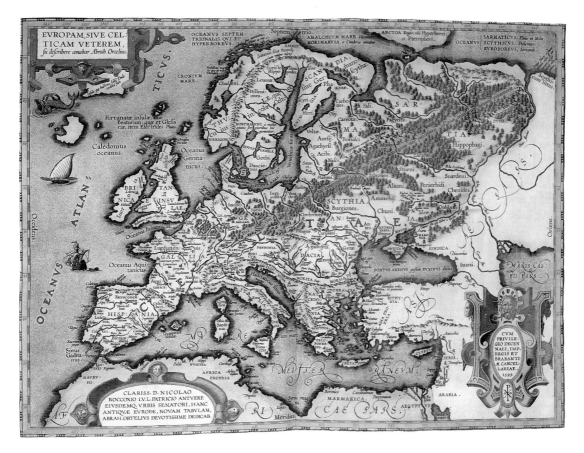

EVROPAM, SIVE CEL=
TICAM VETEREM,
sic describere conabar Abrah. Ortelius.

CLARISS. D. NICOLAO
ROCCOXIO I.V.L. PATRICIO ANTVERP.
EIVSDEMQ. VRBIS SENATORI, HANC
ANTIQVÆ EVROPÆ, NOVAM TABVLAM,
ABRAH. ORTELIVS DEVOTISSIME DEDICAB.

CVM
PRIVILE-
GIO DECEN-
NALI, IMP.
REGIS ET
BRABANTI-
Æ CANCEL-
LARIAE.
1595

MAPS OF THE ANCIENT WORLD

CELTIC EUROPE

Abraham Ortelius, in *Parergon*, Antwerp, 1595
Osher Collection, University of Southern Maine

This map depicts Europe during the period of Celtic dominance. Between the sixth and third centuries B.C., the Celts, a group of barbarian tribes from central Europe, conquered a vast region extending from Iberia to the Black Sea. They were driven back and defeated by the Romans in the third and second centuries B.C.

Pomegranate, Box 6099, Rohnert Park, CA 94927

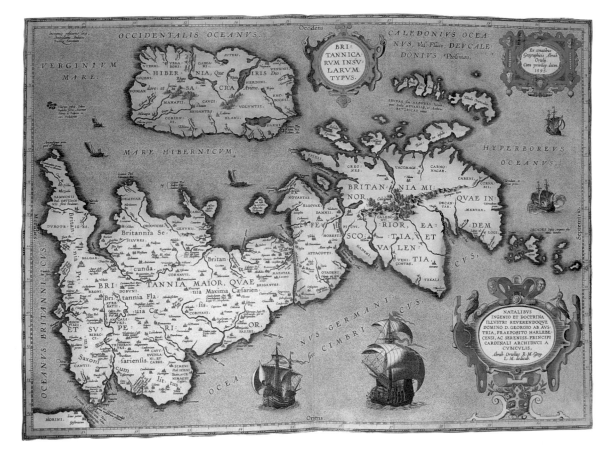

MAPS of the ANCIENT WORLD

THE BRITISH ISLES IN ROMAN TIMES

Abraham Ortelius, in *Parergon*, Antwerp, 1595
Osher Collection, University of Southern Maine

This map, oriented with north to the right, contains place names
from the Roman period. Ireland is Hibernia, England is Britannia
Maior and Scotland is Britannia Minor or Scotia. The Scottish
highlands are Caledonia, and London is Londinum Augusta. An
inscription adjacent to London indicates the point at which
Caesar crossed the Thames (Tamesis) River.

Pomegranate, Box 6099, Rohnert Park, CA 94927

PANNONIAE, ET ILLYRICI VETERIS TABVLA.

Ex conatibus geographicis Abrahami Ortelij Antverpiani.

Cum Gratia et Privilegio decennali 1590.

MAPS OF THE ANCIENT WORLD

ANCIENT DALMATIA

Abraham Ortelius, in *Parergon*, Antwerp, 1595
Osher Collection, University of Southern Maine

Shown here are the Roman provinces of Pannonia and Illyria
(Illyris), occupying the east coast of the Adriatic Sea and the
adjacent Balkan regions. Several Roman emperors, for example
Diocletian, were natives of Illyria. The text panel at the lower left
lists ancient tribes and places whose locations were unknown.

Pomegranate, Box 6099, Rohnert Park, CA 94927

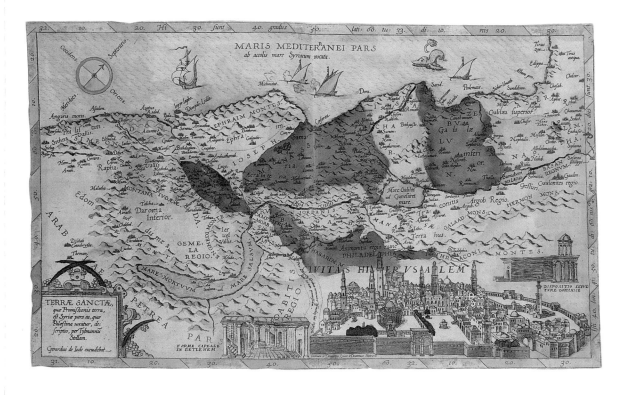

MAPS of the ANCIENT WORLD

HOLY LAND

Gerard de Jode, in *Speculum Orbis Terrarum*,
Antwerp, 1578

Smith Collection, University of Southern Maine

West is at the top. A detailed bird's-eye view of the walled city of
Jerusalem is seen at the lower right, depicted as it would have
appeared to a contemporary pilgrim, with the Dome of the Rock
on the former site of Solomon's Temple. The view is flanked by
vignettes of the Church of the Holy Sepulchre (above and to the
right) and the Chapel of the Nativity in Bethlehem (to the left).

Pomegranate, Box 6099, Rohnert Park, CA 94927

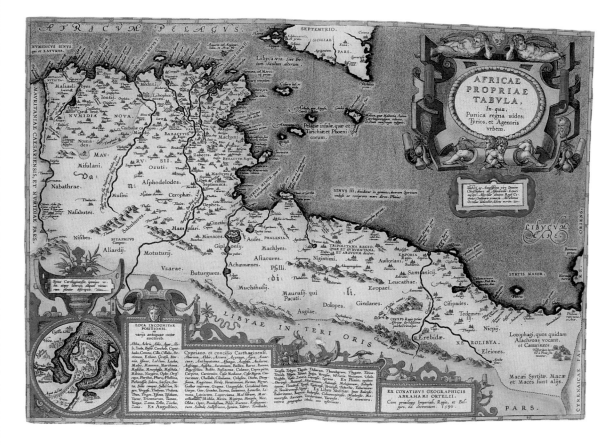

MAPS OF THE ANCIENT WORLD

ANCIENT NORTH AFRICA

Abraham Ortelius, in *Parergon*, Antwerp, 1595
Osher Collection, University of Southern Maine

Phoenician colonies on the northern coast of Africa are seen here, the most important of which was Carthage, established by sea-farers from the kingdom of Tyre. The inset in the lower left corner contains a plan of the ancient walled city of Carthage, destroyed by the Romans during the Third Punic War.

Pomegranate, Box 6099, Rohnert Park, CA 94927

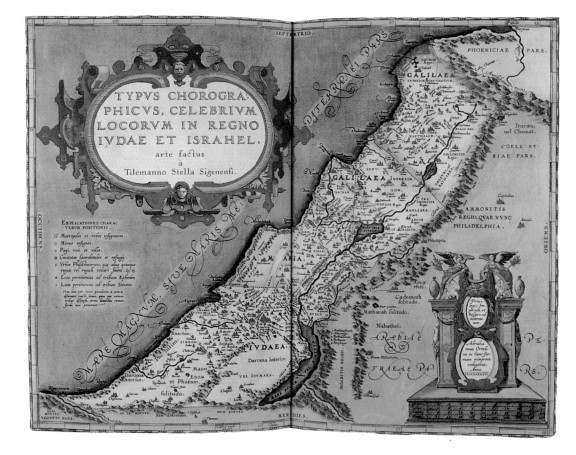

MAPS OF THE ANCIENT WORLD

KINGDOMS OF JUDAH AND ISRAEL

Abraham Ortelius, in *Parergon*, Antwerp, 1595

Osher Collection, University of Southern Maine

This Ortelius map of the Holy Land is the most detailed of that region, depicting "the most important places in the Kingdoms of Judah and Israel." Both sides of the Jordan River are included within the boundaries of Palestine. The map is embellished by two ornate baroque cartouches.

Pomegranate, Box 6099, Rohnert Park, CA 94927

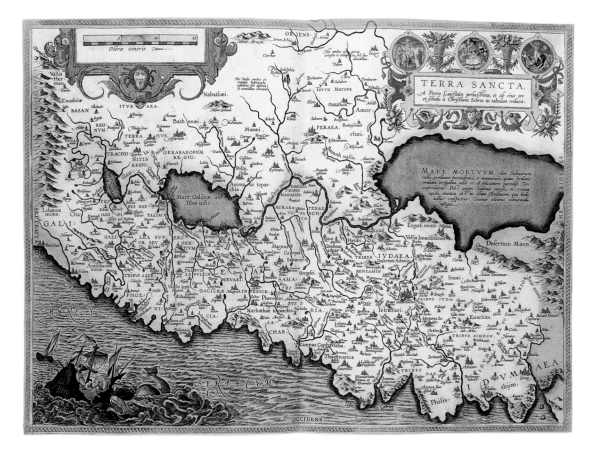

MAPS OF THE ANCIENT WORLD

HOLY LAND

Abraham Ortelius, in *Theatrum Orbis Terrarum*, Antwerp, 1595

Osher Collection, University of Southern Maine

This is Ortelius's second Holy Land map, made in 1584 and oriented with east at the top. It contains numerous biblical place names along with embellishments derived from both the Old and New Testaments. At the lower left Jonah is being thrown to a ferocious, fishlike whale. Medallions above the title cartouche depict, from left to right, the Crucifixion, the Nativity and the Resurrection.

Pomegranate, Box 6099, Rohnert Park, CA 94927

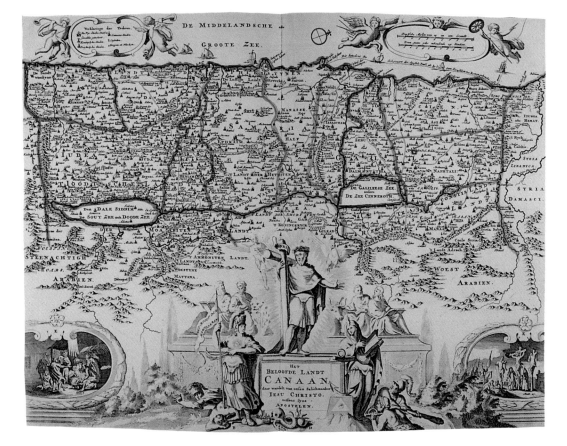

MAPS of the ANCIENT WORLD

THE PROMISED LAND CANAAN
Maker unknown; from a Dutch Bible
[seventeenth century]
Smith Collection, University of Southern Maine

During the sixteenth century it became customary to include
maps in Bibles, and by the seventeenth century a standard
complement of five or six maps based on the Old and New
Testaments was traditional. This is a typical example, for the
Book of Matthew, showing the territorial distribution of the
Twelve Tribes and, in the lower corners, scenes of the Nativity
and the Crucifixion.

Pomegranate, Box 6099, Rohnert Park, CA 94927

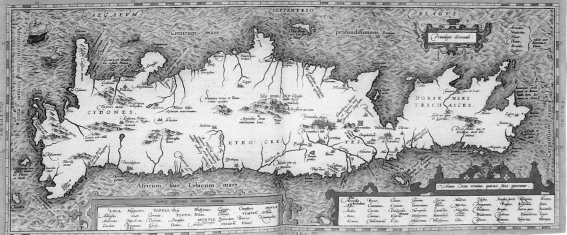

MAPS OF THE ANCIENT WORLD

ANCIENT CRETE, CORSICA AND SARDINIA
Abraham Ortelius, in *Parergon*, Antwerp, 1595
Osher Collection, University of Southern Maine

Three of the larger Mediterranean islands are depicted here,
along with the smaller islands of the Ionian Sea, as they were
known in ancient times. While many topographical features and
settlements are delineated, gaps in historical and geographic
knowledge are noted in the panels at the bottom, which list
places and cities whose locations were uncertain or unknown.

Pomegranate, Box 6099, Rohnert Park, CA 94927

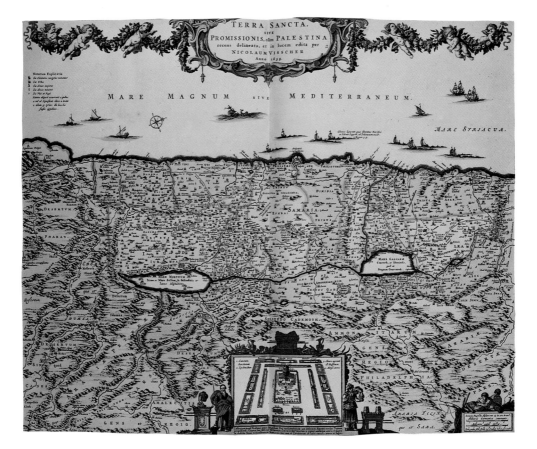

TERRA SANCTA,
SIVE
PROMISSIONIS, olim PALESTINA
recens delineata, et in lucem edita per
NICOLAUM VISSCHER
Anno 1659.

Notarum Explicatio

MARE   MAGNUM   SIVE   MEDITERRANEUM.

MARE SYRIACUM.

DESERTUM

PHARAN.

SAMARIA

MARE GALILÆ

SILE MORTUUM

SOLITUDO CADEMOTH

AMMONITARUM

GENS et REGIO.

PHILADELPHIA

ARABIA FELIX
que et SABA.

MAPS OF THE ANCIENT WORLD

HOLY LAND

Nicolas Visscher I; from Nicolas Visscher II,
Atlas Minor, Amsterdam, c. 1689
Smith Collection, University of Southern Maine

Oriented to the west, this map contains a wealth of Old
Testament information, including the tribal divisions, towns
and even caves and tombs. At the bottom center is a plan of the
encampment at Mount Sinai, showing the Tabernacle in the
center, surrounded by the Twelve Tribes. Moses is depicted at
the left and Aaron at the right; the Golden Ark is at the top, and
holy vessels are at either side.

Pomegranate, Box 6099, Rohnert Park, CA 94927

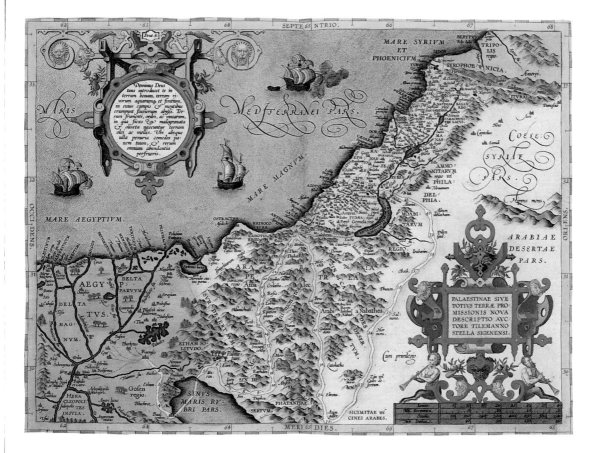

MAPS OF THE ANCIENT WORLD

PALESTINE

Abraham Ortelius, in *Parergon*, Antwerp, 1595
Osher Collection, University of Southern Maine

This is Ortelius's first map of the Holy Land, originally produced
for the 1570 edition of his world atlas. Covering "the entire Holy
Land" from the Nile Delta to Beirut, it depicts the route of the
Exodus from Egypt across the Red Sea, tracing the wanderings
of the Israelites in the desert wilderness and their eventual arrival
in the Promised Land.

Pomegranate, Box 6099, Rohnert Park, CA 94927

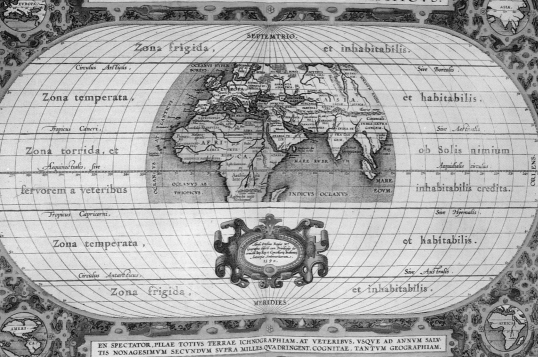

AEVI VETERIS, TYPVS GEOGRAPHICVS.

SEPTEMTRIO.

Zona frigida, et inhabitabilis.

Circulus Arcticus, Sive Borealis.

Zona temperata, et habitabilis.

Tropicus Cancri, Sive Aestivalis

Zona torrida, et ob Solis nimium

Aequinoctialis, sive Aequidialis circulus

fervorem a veteribus inhabitabilis credita.

Tropicus Capricorni, Sive Hyemalis.

Zona temperata, et habitabilis.

Circulus Antarcticus, Sive Australis.

Zona frigida, et inhabitabilis.

MERIDIES.

OCCIDENS.

ORIENS.

EN SPECTATOR, PILAE TOTIVS TERRAE ICHNOGRAPHIAM. AT VETERIBVS, VSQVE AD ANNVM SALV-
TIS NONAGESIMVM SECVNDVM SVPRA MILLES.QVADRINGENT.COGNITAE, TANTVM GEOGRAPHIAM.

MAPS OF THE ANCIENT WORLD

THE CLASSICAL ANCIENT WORLD

Abraham Ortelius, in *Parergon*, Antwerp, 1595
Osher Collection, University of Southern Maine

The ancient world of the classical Greeks and Romans is seen
here, framed within an oval projection outlining the limits of the
earth as known at the time of Ortelius. The five "climatic" zones
are delineated—two "frigida," two "temperata" and a single
"torrida." It is noted that the "Zona torrida" was believed by the
ancients to be uninhabitable because of excessive solar heat. The
southern "Zona temperata," as yet unexplored and unknown, is
nevertheless clearly designated as habitable. Corner medallions
within the ornamental strapwork border contain late-sixteenth-
century depictions of the four continents.

Pomegranate, Box 6099, Rohnert Park, CA 94927